THE SIMPLE ABUNDANCE

JOURNAL OF GRATITUDE

SARAH BAN BREATHNACH

WARNER
BOOKS

A TIME WARNER COMPANY

Simple Abundance®
is a registered trademark of Sarah Ban Breathnach

Warner Books, Inc.,
1271 Avenue of the Americas, New York, NY 10022

 A Time Warner Company

Printed in the United States of America
First Printing: November 1996
10 9 8 7 6 5 4 3 2 1

ISBN: 0-446-52106-X

DESIGN BY KATHLEEN HERLIHY-PAOLI, INKSTONE DESIGN

IF THE ONLY PRAYER
YOU EVER SAY
IN YOUR ENTIRE LIFE
IS THANK YOU,
IT WILL BE ENOUGH.

—MEISTER ECKHART

For Oprah
with love

THANK YOU.

SIMPLE ABUNDANCE

Good, the more Communicated,
more abundant grows.

—JOHN MILTON

There is a wonderful Hasidic parable about the power of gratitude to change the course of our destiny in a heartbeat, the speed, I imagine, it takes for a "thank you" to reach Heaven's ears.

Once times were tough. Two men—both poor farmers—were walking down a country lane and met their Rabbi. "How is it for you?" the Rabbi asked the first man. "Lousy," he grumbled, bemoaning his lot and lack. "Terrible, hard, awful. Not worth getting out of bed for. Life is lousy."

Now, God was eavesdropping on this conversation. "Lousy?" the Almighty thought. "You think your life is lousy now, you ungrateful lout? I'll show you what lousy is."

Then the Rabbi turned to the second man. "And you, my friend?"

"Ah, Rabbi—life is good. God is so gracious, so generous. Each morning when I awaken, I'm so grateful for the gift of another day, for I know, rain or shine, it will unfold in wonder and blessings too bountiful to count. Life is so good."

God smiled as the second man's thanksgiving soared upwards until it became one with the harmony of the heavenly hosts. Then the Almighty roared with delighted laughter. "Good? You think your life is good now? I'll show you what *good* is!"

Gratitude is the most passionate transformative force in the cosmos. When we offer thanks to God or to another human being, gratitude gifts us with renewal, reflection, reconnection. Gratitude bestows reverence, allowing us to encounter everyday epiphanies, those transcendent moments of awe that change forever how we experience life (is it abundant or is it lacking?) and the world (is it friendly or is it hostile?). Once we accept that abundance and lack are parallel realities and that each day we choose—consciously or unconsciously—which world we will inhabit, a deep inner shift in our reality occurs. We discover the sacred in the ordinary and we realize that every day is literally a gift. How we conduct our daily round, how we celebrate it, cherish it and consecrate it is how we express our thankfulness to the Giver of all good.

Gratitude holds us together even as we're falling apart. Ironically, gratitude's most powerful mysteries are often revealed when we are struggling in the midst of personal turmoil. When we stumble in the darkness, rage in anger, hurl faith across the room, abandon all hope. While we cry ourselves to sleep, gratitude waits patiently to console and reassure us; there is a landscape larger than the one we can see.

It's easy to be grateful when life hums—when the money's in the bank, the romance is divine and you're healthy. But when you don't know how the bills will get paid, or he doesn't love you back or she won't return your calls or you're reeling from a devastating diagnosis, "thank you" usually isn't the phrase that immediately comes to mind.

At least it wasn't for me (or isn't always—the currents of consciousness ebb and flow around here). But after having been on the Simple Abundance path for the last five years and having been "loved into full being" (as the poet Elizabeth Barrett Browning so beautifully puts it) by gratitude, I know what I need to do if I am to remain centered, especially when fortune's tumultuous cycles of change throw me for a loop. I must *stop* focusing on what's lacking in my life and bring my complete attention to all that I have—the "simple abundance" that surrounds us all. Small acts of kindness heal even the deepest wounds; savoring fleeting moments of comfort restores serenity.

But we don't feel grateful when our hearts are broken and our dreams are dashed. However, it has been my experience that it doesn't really matter how we *feel*, what matters is that we just *do* it. The Bible instructs us "to give thanks in all circumstances," but it doesn't tell us we have to be smiling while we say it. In fact, I suspect that the "thank you's" offered in the depths of despair are the most treasured because they are priceless tokens of trust, especially when trusting Spirit is the last thing in the world you want to do.

Once during a season of profound loss I forced out a sarcastic litany of "thanks" because I knew it was the only way I could mourn and move on (the downside to enlightenment no one ever mentions is that once you understand how the Universe operates, you can't play dumb). "There, I've *thanked* you for my misery and pain. Are you happy now? But don't you dare come near me," I cried, holding up my hand to Heaven in defiance, pushing away the Love I needed most. "So thanks a million. Now go your way, and I'll go mine."

Naked, complete, bitter surrender. But only because I was beaten senseless by sorrow. Sometimes in order to give us our highest good, Spirit takes no prisoners. Almost immediately I was enwrapped in a surreal sense of peace which certainly passed my feeble capacity for understanding. I became genuinely grateful to have been carried off the battlefield of disbelief by a Source of power, wisdom, strength and love far greater than my own. Within a few days the trajectory of my life was forever altered in miraculous ways. *First the gesture, then the grace.*

But gratitude's most profound lessons are revealed through glimmers of joy. People often ask me what is *Simple Abundance*'s greatest gift to me, for there have been, and continue to be, so many blessings. If I can choose only one, it is that finally, after a lifetime of searching, I have been reunited with my soul mate. I have fallen passionately in love with Life—despite all its complexities, compromises and contradictions—and Life has fallen passionately in love with me, in spite of mine. Believe me, you will never find a lover who will adore, desire, caress, embrace, and delight you more than Real Life. Gratitude was our matchmaker and it can be yours as well.

This is why I wanted to create a special journal—a combination love letter and ledger of largesse—so that you might also bear witness to the goodness and generosity of your soul mate. At the heart of the Simple Abundance journey is an authentic awakening: you already possess all you need to be genuinely happy. All you truly need is the awareness of all you have. Today. Not tomorrow, or next week or next year. Gratitude spiritually induces this awakening with a lover's kiss.

Some days filling your gratitude journal will be easy. Other days the only thing you might be thankful for is that the day is over. That's okay—all loving relationships experience rough patches. But you still need four more entries, which is why I've included a list of over one hundred often overlooked blessings to inspire you to search for the minor as well as the major chords of contentment. If you give thanks for five gifts every day, in two months you will not look at your life in the same way as you might now. Gratitude can lead you, as it did me, away from the darkness of complicated need into the Light of Simple Abundance.

I have often wondered, what if, after the Fall, Adam and Eve returned to Eden's gate just to say: "Thank You. We blew it because we wanted it all and didn't appreciate how much we already had been given. But we just needed You to know how grateful we truly are. Our idyll was brief but our rapture knew no bounds. We were so blessed. Thank you, thank you, thank you. We'll carry and cherish these precious memories of exquisite pleasure and bliss within our souls throughout all of eternity."

Do you think God would have let them back into Paradise?

I do.

Because every time we remember to say "thank you" we experience nothing less than Heaven on earth.

Sarah Ban Breathnach

NOVEMBER 1996

150 Often Overlooked Blessings

Faith. Faith in a Spirit possessing greater strength, wisdom, power, and love than you do. Faith in the ultimate goodness of Life. Faith in yourself. Faith that as you seek, you will find.

The dream that will not die because you were born to love it into full being.

Answered prayers.

The kindness of strangers.

The warmth and security of home. Crossing the threshold and closing the door after a hard day.

Expressions of unconditional love and support.

Your health. The health of those you love.

That moment of relief when you realize that the pain has subsided.

A job that provides steady income while you pursue your dreams.

Feeling the presence of Spirit in your life.

Sinking into a warm, softly scented bath after a stressful day.

The aroma of something delicious wafting from the kitchen.

Not having to cook tonight.

Your boundless imagination.

When hope is restored.

Following your intuition and being delighted that you did.

Daydreams. Reveries. Textured, technicolor nightscapes of happiness and good fortune that have you awakening with a smile.

Twelve hours uninterrupted sleep.

Breakfast in bed.

Serenity as you pay bills.

Acceptance after struggle.

Seeing him or her and having your heart skip a beat.

Seeing him or her and finally feeling nothing.

Completely and utterly surrendering to *what is* and then waiting expectantly for the good that is to come.

An afternoon to do as you please.

Doing a great job and having it and your efforts appreciated.

Holding your child in your arms.

Delighting in other people's children.

Witnessing the birth of new life.

The times when your ideas "clicked" with others.

The fragrance of a vacation day.

The beach. The feel of the sand beneath your feet, the salty breeze, the warming rays of the sun.

A walk in the woods and becoming aware of life all around you.

Trying something new and loving it.

The desire for knowledge.

Two hours in a wonderful bookstore.

Waking up early enough to watch the sun rise with a cup of tea or coffee.

Watching the sunset.

Meeting a kindred spirit.

Meeting your soul mate(s) and recognizing that you have known each other before.

The moment when the veil is lifted from both your eyes and you know that you know.

Hearing a piece of music that instantly touches your soul.

Being able to add that music to your collection immediately.

Reading a passage in a book or a poem that expresses exactly how you feel.

Memorizing a beautiful piece of poetry and sharing it with another in conversation.

Holding hands.

Having a congenial conversation with a stranger on a plane, train, or bus.

Successfully hailing a cab in rush hour.

A nap.

Realizing that there are no coincidences.

Nailing the punch line in a favorite joke. Hearing their laughter.

Relishing a wonderful movie. Liking it so much you want to see it again as the credits roll. Seeing it again.

Laughing so hard, you can't catch your breath and your sides ache.

The sacred release of a good cry.

Bringing joy, happiness, and comfort to another person or creature.

The loyal, loving companionship of pets.

Feeling you're part of a loving and supportive community or church.

Finding a parking space exactly when you need one.

Summoning up the courage to surmount a challenge.

Taking tiny and big risks and having them pay off.

Investing time, creative energy, and emotion in yourself, then reaping the rich harvest of authentic success sown by Love.

Coming in after being caught in a soaking thunderstorm, getting out of wet clothes and becoming warm and dry.

Meeting a deadline.

Making it to the game just in time to see her hit her first home run.

Friendship that endures and thrives despite the obstacles of time and distance.

Being able to trust another human being.

The experience of a pleasant déjà vu. The moment you realize it doesn't have to be déjà vu all over again unless you want it to.

Wisdom gleaned through life experiences (both yours and others). Knowing how to use it.

Speaking another language.

Reading a book that changes your life.

Receiving flowers.

Moving on.

Letting go gracefully without regrets.

The first morsel of your favorite comfort food.

Savoring the scents of life (flowers, food, your lover, the earth, your child's hair).

The fresh feeling that immediately comes after a shower and washing your hair.

Being able to travel; the adventure of new places.

Room service.

The support and loving presence of sisters and/or brothers.

Achieving a long sought after goal. The moment when your accomplishment emotionally registers.

Feeling a sense of pride in yourself.

Wishing upon a star. Having your wish come true.

Finding your perfect scent.

Making eye contact and smiling with a gorgeous stranger.

A dance partner who makes you feel like Ginger Rogers (or Fred Astaire).

That person who takes your breath away when you are near or feel him or her next to you.

The first kiss.

Being with a person with whom you can communicate without words.

The moment you realize you'd marry your spouse all over again.

Sharing the holidays with people you really want to be with.

Easily switching carpool days.

Finding, having and wearing something that makes you feel special.

Saying "no" to the bake sale without guilt.

A miracle.

Bargains at thrift shops, flea markets, garage sales.

The sense of relief throwing stuff out brings.

Your mentor.

The individual who inspired your career and made you believe that there is nothing as real as a dream.

The person who believed in you when you weren't able to believe in yourself.

A fortune cookie with just the right message.

The precious lingering memory of your mother's sweet scent. The comforting memory of your father's hand.

Being able to provide for the needs and wants of your loved ones.

The moment you are able to distinguish between your needs and your wants.

Watching others enjoy your creations, whether it's a meal, flowers from your garden, or a pair of pants you just ironed.

Being able to make clear, conscious, creative choices.

Air-conditioning on an excruciatingly hot and humid day.

Bring upgraded to first class.

The contentment of sitting before a roaring fire on a winter's evening.

Receiving a love letter. Writing one.

All of the tragedy you and yours have escaped.

Becoming fascinated in a subject and learning more about it.

Hearing the words "I love you."

The awareness of innocence.

The long awaited phone call with good news.

When the repair bill is less than you'd expected.

A sense of humor during good and rough patches.

Not losing your temper.

Giving and receiving forgiveness after a painful estrangement.

Perfect timing.

Fitting into last year's clothes.

Knowing a favorite book awaits you at the end of a day.

Sleeping on the perfect pillow. The contentment of being wrapped in a favorite blanket, quilt, or goose-down comforter.

Sharing your aspirations for the future with a close friend.

Reawakening an old passion; discovering a new one.

The haven of a comforting shoulder to cry on; the warming embrace of a loved one.

Pampering yourself.

Listening to the whispers of your authentic self and taking her or his advice.

The generosity and hospitality of good neighbors.

Family and friends who remember funny or uplifting stories about your past that you've forgotten and share them with you.

Finding a lost pet.

Rediscovering old family photos.

Playing hooky.

The intimate bond of friendship that protects, nurtures, inspires, and comforts.

The man or woman in your life who is neither a past nor present love but simply a precious friend who adores you.

Waking up to a perfectly beautiful day for a planned outdoor event.

Working with people you enjoy being around. Working with people who are pleasant, kind, funny, considerate, and who honor your contribution.

An opportunity to interview for the dream job. Getting it.

Receiving the *perfect* gift. Finding one for someone else.

Catching a glimpse of yourself in the mirror and delighting in what you see.

Having your child appreciate your sense of humor.

An unexpected compliment that makes your day.

Enjoying the company of smart, witty, savvy people, delighting in stimulating conversation and holding your own.

Completing the crossword puzzle without help.

Looking fabulous at your class reunion.

Listening to the oldies and recalling happy moments.

A rare, relaxing break with your co-worker during a hectic day.

Paying off your credit card balance.

Coming up with the perfect retort at the moment you need it and not two hours later.

The sound of raindrops on your roof at night.

Friends and family who can both truly rejoice with you and console in times of sorrow.

JANUARY

2010

YOU ONLY LIVE
ONCE–
BUT IF YOU WORK IT RIGHT,
ONCE IS ENOUGH.

—JOE E. LEWIS

I'll try to keep it up.
Received this Good will
Feb 12th 2010.

Gratitude unlocks the fullness of life. It turns what we have into enough, and more. It turns denial into acceptance, chaos to order, confusion to clarity. It can turn a meal into a feast, a house into a home, a stranger into a friend. Gratitude makes sense of our past, brings peace for today, and creates a vision for tomorrow.
—MELODY BEATTIE

JANUARY 1

JANUARY 2

JANUARY 3

JANUARY 4

....

....

....

....

....

JANUARY 5

....

....

....

....

....

JANUARY 6

....

....

....

....

....

JANUARY 7

....

....

....

....

....

January 8

....

....

....

....

....

January 9

....

....

....

....

....

January 10

....

....

....

....

....

January 11

....

....

....

....

....

Gratitude helps you to grow and expand; gratitude brings joy and laughter into your life and into the lives of all those around you.

—EILEEN CADDY

JANUARY 12

JANUARY 13

JANUARY 14

Just to be is a blessing. Just to live is holy.

—RABBI ABRAHAM HESCHEL

JANUARY 15

JANUARY 16

JANUARY 17

JANUARY 18

....

....

....

....

....

JANUARY 19

....

....

....

....

JANUARY 20

....

....

....

....

JANUARY 21

....

....

....

....

JANUARY 22

....

....

....

....

....

JANUARY 23

....

....

....

....

JANUARY 24

....

....

....

....

....

JANUARY 25

....

....

....

....

....

Gratitude is our most direct line to God and the angels. If we take the time, no matter how crazy and troubled we feel, we can find something to be thankful for. The more we seek gratitude, the more reason the angels will give us for gratitude and joy to exist in our lives.

—TERRY LYNN TAYLOR

JANUARY 26

Two new class of A R E - E. statest, net about 9 new souls! Hope this will be good outcome? neet every 2 wks,

JANUARY 27

JANUARY 28

Let's choose today to quench our thirst for the "good life" we think others lead by acknowledging the good that already exists in our own lives. We can then offer the Universe the gift of our grateful hearts.

—S.B.B.

JANUARY 29

....

....

....

....

....

JANUARY 30

....

....

....

....

....

JANUARY 31

....

....

....

....

....

FEBRUARY

LOVE WHOLEHEARTEDLY,

BE SURPRISED,

GIVE THANKS AND PRAISE–

THEN

YOU WILL DISCOVER

THE FULLNESS

OF YOUR LIFE.

—BROTHER DAVID STEINDL-RAST

Gratitude is a twofold love—love coming to visit us, and love running out to greet a welcome guest.

—Henry Van Dyke

February 1

....

....

....

....

....

February 2

....

....

....

....

....

February 3

....

....

....

....

....

February 4

....
....
....
....
....

February 5

....
....
....
....
....

February 6

....
....
....
....
....

February 7

....
....
....
....
....

FEBRUARY 8

FEBRUARY 9

Snowed- so class cancelled?

FEBRUARY 10

FEBRUARY 11

Ann called Jody + changed 2/14
am glad,
I know she needs effagier + I
need Pacale Too,

Let your heart be awakened to the transforming
power of gratefulness.

—S.B.B.

FEBRUARY 12

"M" B.day - she called + we'll celebrate
next WK.son. went To Botlt '6' + Arny
good results, very grateful - Beautiful day+ evening.

FEBRUARY 13

FEBRUARY 14 2010

Sue P.M. Judy + I to on argan +
bell consert I 1st Lu + H. Wodder-
ful day + evening, Saw Sean +
Emily Perform - great kids !!

There is a calmness to a life lived in Gratitude, a quiet joy.

—RALPH H. BLUM

FEBRUARY 15

FEBRUARY 16

FEBRUARY 17

FEBRUARY 18

FEBRUARY 19

FEBRUARY 20

I took L. out For Her BD. - AAnies
So Beloit Delecious + Had
Leftovers

FEBRUARY 21

all went well at n.n. lost nite, but no
Emily July WASS uPPosed To be consing
Home No s How!

God has two dwellings; one in heaven, and the other in a meek and thankful heart.

—Izaak Walton

February 22

February 23

Class next was good,
++ P. T. was around!

February 24

February 25

....
....
....
....
....

February 26

....
....
....
....
....

February 27

....
....
....
....
....

February 28

....
....
....
....
....

Grace is available for each of us every day—our spiritual daily bread—but we've got to remember to ask for it with a grateful heart and not worry about whether there will be enough for tomorrow.

—S.B.B.

FEBRUARY 29

....

....

....

....

....

MARCH

ONLY WHEN WE
ARE NO LONGER AFRAID
DO WE BEGIN TO
LIVE IN EVERY EXPERIENCE,
PAINFUL OR JOYOUS,
TO LIVE IN GRATITUDE
FOR EVERY MOMENT,
TO LIVE ABUNDANTLY.

—DOROTHY THOMPSON

Feeling grateful or appreciative of someone or something in your life actually attracts more of the things that you appreciate and value into your life. And, the more of your life that you like and appreciate, the healthier you'll be. Science is now documenting what women have known intuitively for millennia: that "thinking with your heart" will lead you in the right direction.

—CHRISTIANE NORTHRUP, M.D.

MARCH 1

MARCH 2

MARCH 3

Hday— my PHone died + so we got a new one. Is wonderful but must still lear How To Run iti

MARCH 4

MARCH 5

MARCH 6

Dame K. wrote + she is doing well,
thank Heavens,

MARCH 7

MARCH 8

Diary clerk arrived this month, Betty N. Wrote, must ANSWER Her.

MARCH 9

Class next and 3 + me + Leonard! Very Bored But still grateful also library but did not like it too much.

MARCH 10

MARCH 11

Called Judy's Neighbors & she was in Hospi, How convelest Home getting well.

The first wealth is health.

—RALPH WALDO EMERSON

MARCH 12

....
....
....
....
....

MARCH 13

....
....
....
....
....

MARCH 14

....
....
....
....
....

For today and its blessings, I owe the world an attitude of gratitude.
— CLARENCE E. HODGES

MARCH 15

MARCH 16

MARCH 17

MARCH 18

....

....

....

....

....

MARCH 19

....

....

....

....

MARCH 20

....

....

....

....

MARCH 21

....

....

....

....

MARCH 22

....
....
....
....
....

MARCH 23

....
....
....
....
....

MARCH 24

....
....
....
....
....

MARCH 25

....
....
....
....
....

One can never pay in gratitude; one can only pay "in kind" somewhere else in life.

—ANNE MORROW LINDBERGH

MARCH 26

....

....

....

....

....

MARCH 27

....

....

....

....

....

MARCH 28

....

....

....

....

....

True gratitude comes even before the events to which it is related. The gratitude came first, the healing followed.
—THE CHRISTIAN SCIENCE MONITOR

MARCH 29

MARCH 30

MARCH 31

APRIL

TO BE ROOTED

IS PERHAPS THE MOST

IMPORTANT

AND LEAST RECOGNIZED

NEED

OF THE HUMAN SOUL.

—SIMONE WEIL

Cherish your human connections: your relationships with friends and family.

—Barbara Bush

April 1

....
....
....
....
....

April 2

....
....
....
....
....

April 3

....
....
....
....
....

APRIL 4

Easter - Wonderful Day - Took
Jr. To Granite city,

APRIL 5

APRIL 6

APRIL 7

April 8

....
....
....
....
....

April 9

....
....
....
....
....

April 10

....
....
....
....
....

April 11

....
....
....
....
....

Call it a clan, call it a network, call it a tribe, call it a family. Whatever you call it, whoever you are, you need one.

—JANE HOWARD

APRIL 12

APRIL 13

APRIL 14

To speak gratitude is courteous and pleasant, to enact gratitude is generous and noble, but to live gratitude is to touch Heaven.
—JOHANNES A. GAERTNER

APRIL 15

....
....
....
....
....

APRIL 16

....
....
....
....
....

APRIL 17

....
....
....
....
....

APRIL 18

....
....
....
....
....

APRIL 19

....
....
....
....
....

APRIL 20

....
....
....
....
....

APRIL 21

....
....
....
....
....

APRIL 22

....

....

....

....

....

APRIL 23

....

....

....

....

....

APRIL 24

....

....

....

....

....

APRIL 25

....

....

....

....

....

Nothing purchased [can] come close to the renewed sense of gratitude for having family and friends.

—COURTLAND MILLOY

APRIL 26

APRIL 27

APRIL 28

Love is the true means by which the world is enjoyed: our love to others, and others' love to us.

—THOMAS TRAHERNE

APRIL 29

APRIL 30

MAY

A MAN TRAVELS
THE WORLD OVER
IN SEARCH OF
WHAT HE NEEDS
AND
RETURNS HOME
TO FIND IT.

—GEORGE MOORE

Be grateful for the home you have, knowing that at this moment, all you have is all you need.

—S.B.B.

MAY 1

MAY 2

MAY 3

MAY 4

....
....
....
....
....

MAY 5

....
....
....
....
....

MAY 6

....
....
....
....
....

MAY 7

....
....
....
....
....

MAY 8

MAY 9

MAY 10

MAY 11

Walk through the different rooms where you eat, sleep, and live. Bless the walls, the roof, the windows and the foundation. Give thanks for your home exactly as it exists today; sift and sort, simplify, and bring order to the home you have. Realize that the home of your dream dwells within.

—S.B.B.

MAY 12

....

....

....

....

....

MAY 13

....

....

....

....

....

....

MAY 14

....

....

....

....

....

Every spirit builds itself a house, and beyond its house a world, and beyond its world a heaven. Know then that world exists for you.

—RALPH WALDO EMERSON

MAY 15

MAY 16

Grace has graduated — college
we were about 19 for
Supper, we really did'teanyong
except for son Grace
Corion day? Could the ben better

MAY 17

MAY 18

MAY 19

MAY 20

MAY 21

MAY 22

MAY 23

We thee went to church — L, F.
I me + went to brunch
afterword.

MAY 24

MAY 25

The ordinary acts we practice every day at home are of more importance to the soul than their simplicity might suggest.

—THOMAS MOORE

MAY 26

....

....

....

....

MAY 27

....

....

....

....

MAY 28

....

....

....

....

....

We shape our dwellings, and afterwards our dwellings shape us.

—WINSTON CHURCHILL

MAY 29

MAY 30

MAY 31

JUNE

NATURE HAS BEEN

FOR ME,

FOR AS LONG

AS I REMEMBER,

A SOURCE OF SOLACE,

INSPIRATION, ADVENTURE,

AND DELIGHT;

A HOME, A TEACHER,

A COMPANION.

—LORRAINE ANDERSON

Meanings, moods, the whole scale of our inner experience finds in nature the "correspondences" through which we may know our boundless selves.

—KATHLEEN RAINE

JUNE 1

Class tristen - the 3 men
were there but only 2 women
Plus me of course ?
Evening.

JUNE 2

JUNE 3

JUNE 4

Went to G. G. + found Books -
Wonderful - Happy Day

JUNE 5

JUNE 6

mom + Dad were close - it's their
79 wedding Anniversary!
Had dream about my B.D.?
made a supper of left-overs
feel good!

JUNE 7

Did a # of things - feel good
To office in P.M.

JUNE 8

Got Perm — P. M.

JUNE 9

Linda got book Warne
today for 3 weeks —
Pray that works for us.

Marie called & we'll get to get Ha.

JUNE 10

JUNE 11

Read Pecks new Book (To go)
Wonderful, Got His address &
will write him, if I dare.

We learn each day how cultivating gratitude tills the soil of our souls, and then how the seeds of simplicity, order, harmony, beauty, and joy send their roots deep down into the earth of everyday existence.

—S.B.B.

JUNE 12

....
....
....
....
....

JUNE 13

....
....
....
....
....

JUNE 14

....
....
....
....
....

JUNE 15

Post c. From Emily; Had Bad
time of it + so shall quite C.
will write Larry next week. will be
Better than to be Bigotted People)

JUNE 16

JUNE 17

JUNE 18

....

....

....

....

....

JUNE 19

....

....

....

....

....

JUNE 20

....

....

....

....

....

JUNE 21

....

....

....

....

....

JUNE 22

JUNE 23

JUNE 24

JUNE 25

Finished 10 Books &
Turned them in
Library

Both abundance and lack exist simultaneously in our lives, as parallel realities. It is always our conscious choice which secret garden we will tend... when we choose not to focus on what is missing from our lives but are grateful for the abundance that's present—love, health, family, friends, work, the joys of nature and personal pursuits that bring us pleasure—the wasteland of illusion falls away and we experience Heaven on earth.

—S.B.B.

JUNE 26

....

....

....

....

....

JUNE 27

....

....

....

....

....

Study the cycles of Mother Nature, the garden whispers, for they correspond with the cycles of your soul's growth. Quiet your mind. Rope in the restlessness. Be here. Learn to labor. Learn to wait. Learn to wait expectantly. Give thanks for the harvest. Let your harvest be a simply abundant lifestyle rooted not in the world but in Spirit.

—S.B.B.

 SUN JUNE 29

Katy P. Told us she would take us to Tower Hill July 9th T.God for. this went to So Beloit A.n ice cream social,

JUNE 29

JUNE 30

June 28th

JULY

REMEMBER
THAT
NOT TO BE
HAPPY
IS NOT TO BE
GRATEFUL.

—Elizabeth Carter

When we recall the past, we usually find that it is the simplest things—not the great occasions—that in retrospect give off the greatest glow of happiness.

—Bob Hope

July 1

July 2

July 3

JULY 4

Had a Picnic at 40th S. - was
really good, watched fine wks on
my home.

JULY 5

Quiet day - L. worked

JULY 6

JULY 7

Went to see CHicago & A. V. - Very
good.

JULY 8

Hurry H. We are going
Katy called late but did
call - our ride

JULY 9

We leave at noon for Camp
Hope all goes well.
Saw the Surgi in E. Lot
this A.M. He wants me back
in class & Tops!

JULY 10

Was good to wake up at T. H. A Camp.
Went back & antique shopping.
Saw Emily at work in Island
Room.

JULY 11

Don't want to go back Home.
Emily Tucked me in bed this
nite!

Work and live to serve others, to leave the world a little better than you found it and garner for yourself as much peace of mind as you can. This is happiness.

—DAVID SARNOFF

JULY 12

....

....

....

....

JULY 13

....

....

....

....

JULY 14

....

....

....

....

The three grand essentials to happiness in life are something to do, something to love, and something to hope for.

—JOSEPH ADDISON

JULY 15

JULY 16

JULY 17

JULY 18

Finished J. Child Book + made a
receipe for supper — was good.

JULY 19

Will mail letter I have written to E.
I stay at library today to work on
Book.

JULY 20

JULY 21

July 22

....
....
....
....
....

July 23

....
....
....
....
....

July 24

....
....
....
....
....

July 25

....
....
....
....
....

There is no duty we so much underrate as the duty of being happy. By being happy we sow anonymous benefits upon the world.

—ROBERT LOUIS STEVENSON

JULY 26

....
....
....
....
....

JULY 27

....
....
....
....
....

JULY 28

....
....
....
....
....

Happiness is not a possession to be prized. It is a quality of thought, a state of mind.

—DAPHNE DU MAURIER

JULY 29

....
....
....
....
....

JULY 30

....
....
....
....
....

JULY 31

....
....
....
....
....

AUGUST

LET US BE GRATEFUL
TO PEOPLE
WHO MAKE US HAPPY—
THEY ARE THE
CHARMING GARDENERS
WHO MAKE
OUR SOULS BLOSSOM.

—MARCEL PROUST

I awoke this morning with devout thanksgiving for my friends, the old and the new.

—RALPH WALDO EMERSON

AUGUST 1

AUGUST 2

AUGUST 3

AUGUST 4

"L" rented car after her old one stopped,

AUGUST 5

Libertyville called

AUGUST 6

Turned in the last ready list,

AUGUST 7

AUGUST 8

....
....
....
....
....

AUGUST 9

....
....
....
....

AUGUST 10

....
....
....
....
....

AUGUST 11

....
....
....
....
....

Each friend represents a world in us, a world possibly not born until they arrive, and it is only by this meeting that a new world is born.

—ANAÏS NIN

AUGUST 12

AUGUST 13

V. called

AUGUST 14

Called V, Puzzled by Her, Try To find Something To Try To HeIP Her and ~ Prayer + lived,

Friendships begin with liking or gratitude.

—George Eliot

August 15

....

....

....

....

....

August 16

....

....

....

....

....

August 17

....

....

....

....

....

AUGUST 18

AUGUST 19

AUGUST 20

AUGUST 21

Wrote V. & sent various Articles,
we'll see if He is serious, about
Her Problems,

August 22

....

....

....

....

....

August 23

....

....

....

....

....

August 24

....

....

....

....

....

August 25

....

....

....

....

....

Be grateful for the gifts of sharing your earthly span with creatures who comfort. Animals are our spiritual companions, living proof of a simply abundant source of love. None of us feel alone. And if there is a gift, then surely, there must be a Giver.

—S.B.B.

AUGUST 26

AUGUST 27

AUGUST 28

*Your friend is . . . your field which you sow with love
and reap with thanksgiving.*

—KAHLIL GIBRAN

AUGUST 29

....
....
....
....
....

AUGUST 30

....
....
....
....
....

AUGUST 31

....
....
....
....
....

September

THANK GOD
EVERY MORNING
WHEN YOU GET UP
THAT YOU HAVE
SOMETHING
TO DO THAT DAY,
WHICH MUST BE DONE,
WHETHER YOU
LIKE IT OR NOT.

—JAMES RUSSELL LOWELL

To love what you do and feel that it matters—how could anything be more fun?

—KATHARINE GRAHAM

SEPTEMBER 1

....

....

....

....

....

SEPTEMBER 2

....

....

....

....

....

SEPTEMBER 3

....

....

....

....

....

SEPTEMBER 4

....

....

....

....

....

SEPTEMBER 5

....

....

....

....

....

SEPTEMBER 6

....

....

....

....

....

SEPTEMBER 7

....

....

....

....

....

September 8

....
....
....
....
....

September 9

....
....
....
....
....

September 10

....
....
....
....

September 11

....
....
....
....
....

Work is love made visible.

—KAHLIL GIBRAN

SEPTEMBER 12

SEPTEMBER 13

SEPTEMBER 14

The pitcher cries for water to carry and a person for work that is Real.

—MARGE PIERCY

SEPTEMBER 15

....

....

....

....

....

SEPTEMBER 16

....

....

....

....

....

SEPTEMBER 17

....

....

....

....

....

September 18

....

....

....

....

....

September 19

....

....

....

....

....

September 20

....

....

....

....

....

September 21

....

....

....

....

....

SEPTEMBER 22

....
....
....
....
....

SEPTEMBER 23

....
....
....
....
....

SEPTEMBER 24

....
....
....
....
....

SEPTEMBER 25

....
....
....
....
....

Your work is to discover your work and then with all your heart to give yourself to it.

—BUDDHA

SEPTEMBER 26

SEPTEMBER 27

SEPTEMBER 28

#1 Gifts class — we have 15 83
faculters — very interesting

We are made for larger ends than Earth can encompass. Oh, let us be true to our exalted destiny.

—CATHERINE BOOTH

SEPTEMBER 29

....

....

....

....

....

SEPTEMBER 30

....

....

....

....

....

OCTOBER

YEAR BY YEAR
THE COMPLEXITIES
OF THIS SPINNING WORLD
GROW MORE BEWILDERING
AND SO
EACH YEAR WE NEED
ALL THE MORE TO SEEK
PEACE AND COMFORT
IN THE JOYFUL SIMPLICITIES.

—WOMAN'S HOME COMPANION,
DECEMBER 1935

As we become curators of our own contentment on
the Simple Abundance path ... we learn to savor the
small with a grateful heart.
　　　　　　　　　　　　　　　　　　　—S.B.B.

OCTOBER 1

OCTOBER 2

OCTOBER 3

Took Emily to lunch at Lydias

OCTOBER 4

....

....

....

....

....

OCTOBER 5

....

....

....

....

OCTOBER 6

....

....

....

....

OCTOBER 7

....

....

....

....

....

OCTOBER 8

....

....

....

....

....

OCTOBER 9

....

....

....

....

....

OCTOBER 10

....

....

....

....

....

OCTOBER 11

....

....

....

....

....

Once we discover how to appreciate the timeless values in our daily experiences, we can enjoy the best things in life.
—HARRY HEPNER

OCTOBER 12

....

....

....

....

....

OCTOBER 13

....

....

....

....

....

OCTOBER 14

....

....

....

....

....

It isn't the big pleasures that count the most; it's making a great deal out of the little ones.

—JEAN WEBSTER

OCTOBER 15

Linda + I are Partners, I talked too much. Won't do that next time.

OCTOBER 16

OCTOBER 17

Emy to lunch — crop walk

OCTOBER 18

OCTOBER 19

OCTOBER 20

#4 class better than I had thought

OCTOBER 21

OCTOBER 22

....
....
....
....
....

OCTOBER 23

....
....
....
....
....

OCTOBER 24

....
....
....
....
....

OCTOBER 25

....
....
....
....
....

To be really great in little things, to be truly noble and heroic in the insipid details of everyday life, is a virtue so rare as to be worthy of canonization.

—HARRIET BEECHER STOWE

OCTOBER 26

OCTOBER 27

OCTOBER 28

*I am beginning to learn that it is the sweet, simple
things of life which are the real ones after all.*

—LAURA INGALLS WILDER

OCTOBER 29

....
....
....
....
....

OCTOBER 30

....
....
....
....
....

OCTOBER 31

....
....
....
....
....

NOVEMBER

WHATEVER WE ARE
WAITING FOR—PEACE OF MIND,
CONTENTMENT, GRACE,
THE INNER AWARENESS OF
SIMPLE ABUNDANCE—
IT WILL SURELY COME TO US,
BUT ONLY WHEN WE ARE
READY TO RECEIVE IT
WITH AN OPEN
AND GRATEFUL HEART.

—S.B.B.

Gratitude is the inward feeling of kindness received. Thankfulness is the natural impulse to express that feeling. Thanksgiving is the following of that impulse.
—HENRY VAN DYKE

NOVEMBER 1

....

....

....

....

....

NOVEMBER 2

....

....

....

....

....

NOVEMBER 3

....

....

....

....

....

NOVEMBER 4

....

....

....

....

....

NOVEMBER 5

....

....

....

....

....

NOVEMBER 6

....

....

....

....

....

NOVEMBER 7

....

....

....

....

....

November 8

....

....

....

....

....

November 9

....

....

....

....

....

November 10

....

....

....

....

....

November 11

....

....

....

....

....

*Authentic success is being so grateful for the many
blessings bestowed on you and yours that you can
share your portion with others.* —S.B.B.

NOVEMBER 12

....
....
....
....
....

NOVEMBER 13

....
....
....
....
....

NOVEMBER 14

....
....
....
....
....

Let your thanksgiving for all that is rise above the din of disappointment—opportunities lost, mistakes made, the clamor of all that has not yet come.

—S.B.B.

NOVEMBER 15

NOVEMBER 16

NOVEMBER 17

NOVEMBER 18

NOVEMBER 19

NOVEMBER 20

NOVEMBER 21

November 22

....
....
....
....
....

November 23

....
....
....
....
....

November 24

....
....
....
....
....

November 25

....
....
....
....
....

Offer grace for the bounty of goodness. Raise the song of harvest home, the glass of good cheer, the heart overflowing with joy. We have so much for which to be thankful. So much about which to smile, so much to share. So much, that in this season of plenty, we can embrace the season of relinquishment. All we have is all we need. —S.B.B.

NOVEMBER 26

NOVEMBER 27

Gratitude is not only the memory but the homage of the heart rendered to God for his goodness.

—N.P. Willis

November 28

....
....
....
....
....

November 29

....
....
....
....
....

November 30

....
....
....
....
....

DECEMBER

BE READY
AT ALL TIMES
FOR THE
GIFTS OF GOD,
AND ALWAYS
FOR NEW ONES.

—MEISTER ECKHART

*December is all about gifts. Nothing but gifts . . . .
Gifts tied with heartstrings. Gifts that surprise and
delight. Gifts that transform the mundane into the
miraculous. Gifts that nurture the souls of both
the giver and given. Perfect gifts. Authentic gifts. The
gifts of Spirit.*

—S.B.B.

DECEMBER 1

....

....

....

....

....

DECEMBER 2

....

....

....

....

....

DECEMBER 3

....

....

....

....

....

DECEMBER 4

....

....

....

....

....

DECEMBER 5

....

....

....

....

....

DECEMBER 6

....

....

....

....

....

DECEMBER 7

....

....

....

....

....

DECEMBER 8

....
....
....
....
....

DECEMBER 9

....
....
....
....
....

DECEMBER 10

....
....
....
....
....

DECEMBER 11

....
....
....
....
....

Unconditional Love. Selflessness. Trust. Faith.
Forgiveness. Wholeness. Second Chances. Comfort.
Joy. Peace. Reassurance. Rejoicing. Generosity.
Compassion. Charity. Wonder. Acceptance. Courage.
To give such gifts! To truly open our hearts to receive
such gifts gratefully.
　　　　　　　　　　　　　　　　　　　　—S.B.B.

DECEMBER 12

....

....

....

....

....

DECEMBER 13

....

....

....

....

....

DECEMBER 14

....

....

....

....

....

*There is only one real deprivation... and that is not
to be able to give one's gifts to those one loves most.*

—MAY SARTON

DECEMBER 15

....

....

....

....

....

DECEMBER 16

....

....

....

....

....

DECEMBER 17

....

....

....

....

....

DECEMBER 18

....

....

....

....

....

DECEMBER 19

....

....

....

....

....

DECEMBER 20

....

....

....

....

....

DECEMBER 21

....

....

....

....

....

December 22

....

....

....

....

....

December 23

....

....

....

....

....

December 24

....

....

....

....

....

December 25

....

....

....

....

....

God has given us two hands, one to receive with and the other to give with.

—BILLY GRAHAM

DECEMBER 26

....

....

....

....

....

DECEMBER 27

....

....

....

....

....

DECEMBER 28

....

....

....

....

....

Give thanks. Wait. Watch what happens. Get excited. Open your arms as wide as you can to receive all the miracles with your name on them. Godspeed.

—S.B.B.

DECEMBER 29

....

....

....

....

....

DECEMBER 30

....

....

....

....

....

DECEMBER 31

....

....

....

....

....